I0111004

© 2022 Amanda J. Clark. All rights reserved.

No portion of this book may be reproduced in any form without written permission from the publisher or author, except as permitted by U.S. copyright law. For permission contact amanda@disciplingwomen.com.

Published by Divine Appointments Publishing
P.O. Box 41
Allardt, TN 38504

ISBN: 979-8-9875377-0-1

Cover and Illustrations designed by author via Canva.

Visit the author's website at www.disciplingwomen.com

MY DEAREST BEALE,

  I STILL REMEMBER THE VERY MOMENT THE LORD, IN HIS PERFECT TIMING
AND VERY GENTLE SPIRIT, CONFIRMED IN MY HEART THAT HE WANTED TO
BRING YOU INTO THIS WORLD. I KNOW MOMMAS AND DADDIES AREN'T
SUPPOSED TO BE AFRAID, BUT I WAS CERTAINLY LIVING IN FEAR OF THE
UNKNOWNS. I ALSO REMEMBER THAT SAME SPIRIT REMINDING ME THAT
WHAT GOD ASKS ME TO DO, HE WILL NOT LEAVE ME TO DO ON MY OWN.

  SWEET BOY, THESE ARE PROMISES THAT GOD CONTINUES TO USE TO
STRENGTHEN ME. THROUGH YOUR DIAGNOSIS OF A RARE FORM OF BRAIN
CANCER TO A NEW DIAGNOSIS OF A RARE FORM OF EPILEPSY, WE CAN SEE
GOD'S LOVE FOR YOU. HIS LOVE ISN'T A LOVE AS THE WORLD LOVES. HIS
LOVE IS OFTEN REVEALED TO US IN OUR DEEPEST TRIALS. WE HAVE SEEN
GOD'S LOVE CLEARER THAN EVER BEFORE DURING THESE MOST DIFFICULT
TIMES. WE PRAY YOU WILL SEE THE SAME AS YOU GROW IN YOUR
KNOWLEDGE OF HIM.

  WITH THIS NEW EXPERIENCE, WE ARE PRAYING THAT GOD WILL DRAW YOU
TO HIMSELF IN HIS LOVING KINDNESS. IN A FEW SHORT WEEKS, WE HAVE
WATCHED YOU ENDURE MORE THAN MANY WILL EVER HAVE TO ENCOUNTER
DURING THEIR TIME ON EARTH. AS YOUR BEHAVIOR BEGAN TO CHANGE
DRASTICALLY, AND YOU STRUGGLED TO COMMUNICATE WHAT WAS
HAPPENING IN YOUR LITTLE BODY, WE SAW GOD WRITING ANOTHER CHAPTER
IN YOUR STORY. GOD HAS PROVIDED GRACE UPON GRACE AND YOUR DADDA
AND I DESIRE TO ALWAYS REMIND YOU OF THE MERCY HE HAS POURED OUT
UPON YOUR LIFE. YOU ARE LOVED!

MOMMA

BEFORE I EVEN ARRIVED HERE, SHE PRAYED I WOULD KNOW ONE LOVE.

A PERFECT LOVE NOT OF THIS WORLD.

AN EVERLASTING LOVE GIFTED TO ME FROM ABOVE.

John 3:16

WELCOME NEW BABY!

THIS SPECIAL LOVE WAS ONCE A GIFT TO HER, YOU SEE.

THE ONLY WAY SHE COULD SHARE WITH ME, WAS FIRST SHE HAD TO RECEIVE.

MOMMA WASN'T EASILY SURPRISED
BY THE SIN THAT WAS ALREADY AT WORK IN ME.
FOR SHE KNEW SIN IS IN US ALL,
AND I WOULD NEED LOVE TO SET ME FREE.

This LOVE would not come to me only when I'm loveable.
Neither would it run away from me
when I've done something unthinkable.

SHE SPOKE OF THIS LOVE LIKE IT WAS HER OWN.
BUT I HEARD HER TELL OTHERS SHE COULDN'T DO THIS ALONE.

MEMORY VERSE OF THE WEEK:

ROMANS 3:12

MOMMA NEEDED SOMETHING LIKE A SUPERPOWER TO GIVE THIS LOVE TO ME.
I'M NOT ALWAYS THE BEST THAT I CAN BE.

SOME DAYS I AM STUBBORN.
SOME DAYS I'M A HELPER.
SOME DAYS I AM FUNNY.
AND SOME DAYS I'M A YELLER!

I KNEW THIS LOVE MUST BE VERY STRONG.
MANY TIMES SHE WOULD HOLD ME TIGHT AND
SING TO ME THIS SONG:

"I LOVE YOU WHEN YOU'RE GOOD.
I LOVE YOU WHEN YOU'RE MAD.
I LOVE YOU WHEN YOU'RE HAPPY.
AND I LOVE YOU WHEN YOU'RE BAD."

IT MIGHT BE EASY TO THINK THAT NO ONE LOVES ME BETTER THAN MOMMA.
MOST DAYS SHE IS ABLE TO KEEP HER PROMISE.

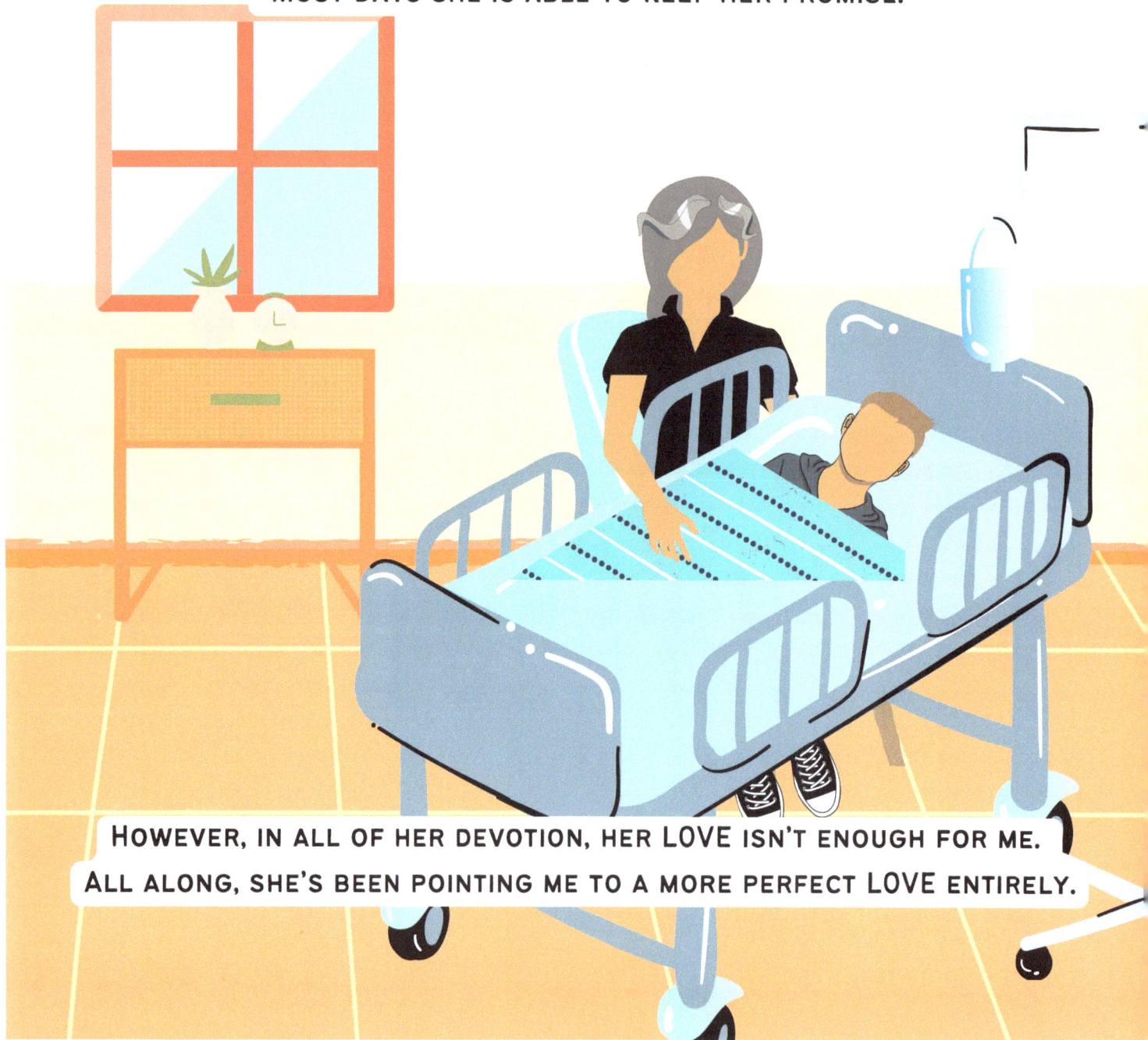

HOWEVER, IN ALL OF HER DEVOTION, HER LOVE ISN'T ENOUGH FOR ME.
ALL ALONG, SHE'S BEEN POINTING ME TO A MORE PERFECT LOVE ENTIRELY.

When Momma sings,
"I LOVE you when you're Good.
I LOVE you when you're Mad.
I LOVE you when you're Happy.
And I LOVE you when you're Bad."

She's creating a desire in my heart to know the One who loves me unconditionally.

THIS LOVE IS SO CONTAGIOUS!
IT SEEMS THAT NO LOVE COULD BE GREATER.

HOW CAN SHE LOVE ME THIS WAY?
EVERY NEW DAY THE SAME? THIS LOVE CAUSES ME TO WANT TO OBEY!

His LOVE can wash away all my sin and make me new from within?
"Momma, please show me more!"

YOU SAY ALL I HAVE TO DO IS BELIEVE. AND ACKNOWLEDGE MY SIN WITH A SINCERE APOLOGY.

"GOD, THANK YOU FOR NOT KEEPING THIS LOVE FROM ME. I'M NOT GOOD, YOU SEE. MY MOMMA LOVES ME SO. NOW, I UNDERSTAND WHY. NOW, I HAVE THE PROMISE THAT I'LL BE WITH YOU WHEN I DIE. UNTIL THEN, SHE WANTS ME TO KNOW YOU AND IN YOUR LOVE GROW."

When momma shows,
"I LOVE you when you're Good.
I LOVE you when you're Mad.
I LOVE you when you're Happy.
And I LOVE you when you're Bad."
That's when Momma LOVES me like JESUS.

Notes:

1. John 3:16
2. Psalm 51:5
3. John 8:36
4. Vincent, Milton. A Gospel Primer for Christians. Focus Publishing 2008. (Page 29)
5. Romans 2:4 and 6:17-18
6. Ephesians 4:24
7. 1 John 1:9
8. Romans 3:12
9. John 14:1-3
10. Ephesians 1:17-19

You Are Loved

God, help me to remember all the special ways Momma loves me. Show me Jesus in each one of them.

NOTES

A portion of sales from this book will go to benefit St. Jude Children's Research Hospital. Our family has been greatly encouraged by our time spent at St. Jude. Since our son's diagnosis in 2017, St. Jude continues to be a resource God uses to prove His faithful provision for us.

At St. Jude Children's Research Hospital families never receive a bill from St. Jude for treatment, travel, housing or food. We will donate $1.00 from the sale of each book. If you would like to make a personal donation, you can visit www.stjude.org.

Thank You

THE CLARK
FAMILY

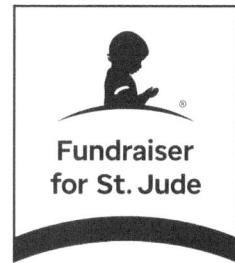

Fundraiser
for St. Jude

www.ingramcontent.com/pod-product-compliance
Lightning Source LLC
LaVergne TN
LVHW072105070426
835508LV00003B/279